Power Pressure Cooker XL Cookbook:

5 Ingredients or Less Quick, Easy & Delicious Electric Pressure Cooker Recipes for Fast & Healthy Meals

By Jamie Mandel

Table of Contents

Introduction

In today's fast-paced society, many people opt to eat out because they are too busy to prepare their own meals. While this option is convenient, constantly eating out prevents you from getting the right nutrition. Moreover, your options are only limited to a few high-fat choices.

So, if you miss eating home-cooked meals without the hassle too much preparation, then using the Power Pressure Cooker XL is your best option. The Power Pressure Cooker XL is a type of third generation of electric pressure cookers that allow you to cook your favorite meals with a single push of a button and within a fraction of a time. Unlike conventional cooking methods, cooking with the Power Pressure Cooker XL allows you to cook your food 70% faster by taking advantage of the high pressure and steam it generates from within the pressure cooker.

The Benefits the Power Pressure Cooker XL

The Power Pressure Cooker XL is a nifty kitchen appliance that can help you prepare delicious meals even if you do not have great cooking skills. But more than preparing sumptuous meals, below are the benefits of adding the Power Pressure Cooker XL to your line of kitchen appliances.

- **Locks in nutrients:** Since food is cooked within an air-tight environment, it locks in the nutrients and flavor of the food so you are eating a more nutrient-dense food compared to conventional cooking.

- **Healthier cooking:** With the Power Pressure Cooker XL, you don't need to add extra fat to make your food flavorful. In fact, it infuses the flavor of whatever food – particularly meat – that you are cooking.

- **Preserves the texture of the vegetables:** Unlike cooking in conventional pressure cookers and cooking methods, vegetables tend to end up having a mushy texture. But with the Power Pressure Cooker, vegetables retain their tender-crisp texture as the fibers are kept intact during the cooking process. This makes food more enjoyable to eat as you can taste different textures while eating.

- **Cooks fast:** You can cut the cooking time into a third when using the Power Pressure Cooker XL so even if you are craving for a pot roast, you don't need to wait for 4 hours to cook it. With this electric pressure cooker, you can make one in as little as 45 minutes.

- **Saves time and energy:** This electric pressure cooker allows you to save time and energy. Since the food is cooked within a short period of time, you don't need to spend too much electricity or gas for cooking. This also translates to savings on your energy bills.

Overall, the Power Pressure Cooker XL is an economical kitchen appliance that allows you to cook your food faster, healthier, and more delicious.

How It Works

The Power Pressure Cooker XL uses a patented Flavor Infusion technology that traps the steam within the pot. The steam forces moisture and liquid into the food thereby looking the intense flavor and nutrients. It is available in both 6-quart and 8-quart units so you can cook your food at different volumes.

The best thing about the Power Pressure Cooker XL is that it has an intelligent one-touch setting that allows you to cook food using pre-set setting so you can never go wrong. There is a pre-set setting for cooking fish, meat, poultry, beans, vegetables, rice, soups, and many others. To cook food, you simply turn the pressure cooker on, select the setting, and attend more important matters.

Another feature of the Power Pressure Cooker XL is its adjustable pressure. You can adjust the pressure from 10 to 80 kPa so that you can cook different types of food perfectly. Moreover, it also has a Keep Warm button that allows you to keep your food warm until you are ready to eat it.

Power Pressure Cooker XL Buttons

Cooking Pre-Set Buttons

The main feature of the Power Pressure Cooker XL is its buttons. But if you are a first-time user, you may probably wonder which button should you choose? As a general rule, select the button that the recipe calls for such that if you are cooking chicken, then press the "meat" button. Below are the different types of cooking buttons available in the Power Pressure Cooker XL. Take note that all pre-set cooking buttons cook food at 7.2 psi.

- **Beans/Lentils:** This button is used to cook beans. The cooking time is pre-set at 5 minutes for soaked beans but you can use the cook time selector to adjust the cooking time to 15 or 30 minutes when cooking dried beans.

- **Fish/Vegetable/Steam:** This button is pre-set for 2 minutes but you can adjust the time selector for 4 or 10 minutes. This is the shortest cooking time available for this type of pressure cooker.

- **Soup/Stew:** The pre-set cooking time for this button is 10 minutes. Use this to make stews and soups. You can adjust the cooking time to 30 or 60 minutes depending on the recipe that you are making.

- **Meat/Chicken:** Whether you are cooking pork, beef, lamb, wild game, or poultry, you only need this pre-set button to cook any type of meat. The pre-set cooking time is at 15 minutes but you can adjust the cooking time to 40 minutes or 60 minutes depending on the size and type of meat.

- **Rice/Risotto:** You can cook risotto and other rice recipes with the Power Pressure Cooker XL. The pre-set cooking time is at 6 minutes for white rice but you can adjust the time to 18 minutes or 25 minutes if you are cooking brown rice and wild rice, respectively.

Additional Buttons

There are other buttons that are included in the Power Pressure Cooker XL. These buttons allow you to extend the functionality of the Power Pressure Cooker XL. Below are the additional buttons that you can see on your Power Pressure Cooker XL.

- **Canning:** Unlike other types of electric pressure cooker, the Power Pressure Cooker XL comes with the canning button. This type of button allows you to can and preserve foods at 12 psi, which is an extremely high pressure. You can use this button not only for canning but for cooking food that requires longer cooking time. You can adjust the cook time to 45 minutes or 120 minutes.

- **Slow cook:** The Power Pressure Cooker XL has a slow cooking function that allows you to cook food slowly for up to 2 hours at preset. However, you can also use the cook time selector to 6 hours or 12 hours. This is an extremely helpful button if you are very busy as you can pop in your ingredients in the pressure cooker and your food will be ready by the time you get home.

- **Delay timer:** Another functional button of this pressure cooker, the delay timer button allows you to set the pressure cooker to start cooking your food later during the day. However, this is not advisable if you are going to cook meat because it can spoil easily.

- **Keep Warm/Cancel:** This button allows you to turn off your pressure cooker. Once the pressure cooking time is over, the pressure cooker automatically turns to the keep warm button.

How to Use It

The Power Pressure Cooker XL is very easy to use. If it is your first time to use this electric pressure cooker, you don't need to be overwhelmed with all the buttons that it has. In fact, using it is just putting the ingredients, pressing the right pre-set button, and you are good to go. Although easy and convenient to use, there are certain things that you need to know when cooking with your Power Pressure Cooker XL.

- Plug the Power Pressure Cooker XL in a 120V wall outlet to turn it on. The read out on the control panel should be at 0000.

- Press the preset button that you want and the pressure cooker will start building up pressure to cook the food.

- If you want to change the cooking time, you can override the pre-set temperature setting by choosing the Time Adjustment button. This control panel is located at the center of the exterior pot.

- If you made any mistakes in setting the program, press the "cancel" button and set the right setting that you want for your recipe.

- As the pressure cooker builds up pressure, you can sauté or sear your food. It is important to remember that the Power Pressure Cooker XL, unlike other electric pressure cooker, does not come with the sauté button but you can still sauté ingredients by pressing the recommended cooking button and cooking without the lid on.

- Drop the ingredients in the pressure cooker.

- Put the lid on and make sure that it is locked. Turn the lid in a counter clockwise direction until you hear the "click" sound.

- Check if the steam vent is on the "pressure mode"

so that the pressure cooker can build the pressure. Once the pressure has built up, the lid stays locked on.

- Put the condensation collector so that any moisture that will drip from the valve can be collected and will not damage the exterior of the pressure cooker.

- Never load the inner pot with liquid above the MAX line as the liquid may find its way to the vents that can cause the vent to be blocked.

- Rotate the inner pot so that it properly sits on the heating plate. This allows equal distribution of heat on inner pot.

- Once the cooking time is up, release the pressure by unlocking the steam release valve to release the steam. You can only open the lid if the pressure inside the pot has reduced to normal. The steam vent is the image with a steam coming out with a triangle. When releasing the pressure, avoid any contact with the hot steam as you might get scalded with the hot steam.

Cleaning the Power Pressure Cooker XL

Similar with the ease of use, cleaning the Power Pressure Cooker XL is also a breeze. It does not require any special cleaners to wash the pressure cooker. You can wipe the pressure with a sponge soaked in warm and soapy water. Below are the steps on how to use the Power Pressure Cooker XL.

- Unplug the pressure cooker and allow to cool to room temperature before cleaning to prevent burns.

- Wash the inner pot with soapy water and clean with a soft cloth. Rinse with clean water and towel dry.

- Do not pour cold water in the Power Pressure Cooker XL because it can damage the pot due to the temperature changes.

- Pay extra attention to the lid. The lid is made up of an outer and inner liner with a gasket so make sure that you remove the liner and gasket from the lid. Wash it separately to remove the food bits that have adhered on the lid. Moreover, check for damages as the presence of damages can prevent the pressure cooker from building up enough pressure to cook food.

- Wipe the outer housing with a soft damp cloth. Do not use chemical cleaner or scouring pads when cleaning either the inner pot or outer housing as it can damage the surface of the Power Pressure Cooker XL.

- Check if the float and pressure valves are working properly and remove any debris found within the valves as you might experience problems when it comes to releasing the steam.

Power Pressure Cooker XL FAQs

1.) Is it made from Lead?

Answer: No. It is made from stainless steel.

2.)   Why isn't the lid coming off?

Answer: If the pressure inside the pot is high, the lid is locked in place.

3.)   What is default time?

Answer: Each pre-set button has a default time. It appears on the control panel screen as soon as you press a specific cooking preset button.

4.)   How long does it take for the pressure cooker to reach full pressure?

Answer: The pressure cooker can build pressure between one minute and 17 minutes.

5.)   Is it safe to leave it on even if you are not at home?

Answer: Yes! The pressure cooker has a delayed timer and slow cooker functions that allow you to cook food even if you are not around.

6.)   Can I cook frozen food in the Power Pressure Cooker?

Answer: Yes. But you have to add another 10 minutes if you are cooking frozen meats.

5-Ingredient Recipes for Power Pressure Cooker XL

Breakfast Recipes

Easy-Peasy Apple Cobbler

Serving size: 4

Preparation time: 5 minutes

Cooking time: 4 minutes

Ingredients:

- 4 peeled medium-sized apples, cored and sliced
- 1 teaspoon cinnamon
- ¼ cup honey
- 2 tablespoon melted butter
- 2 cups granola cereal

Instruction:

1. Place a steamer in the Power Pressure Cooker XL.

2. In a heat-proof bowl, mix all ingredients. Toss until well combined.
3. Place an aluminum foil on top of the bowl.
4. Place inside the pressure cooker.
5. Cover the lid.
6. Press the Fish/Vegetable/Steam button and adjust the cooking time to 4 minutes.
7. Release the steam.
8. Serve warm.

Cheesy Potato Mash

Serving size: 2

Preparation time: 5 minutes

Cooking time: 10 minutes

Ingredients:

- 4 large potatoes
- 1 cup milk
- ¼ cup butter
- ½ cup cheddar cheese
- Salt and pepper to taste

Instruction:

1. Place the potatoes inside the Power Pressure Cooker XL.
2. Add 1 cup of water then close the lid.
3. Press the Fish/Vegetable/Steam button and adjust the cooking time to 10 minutes.
4. Release the steam and pressure to get the potatoes out.
5. Peel the potatoes and mash them in a bowl.
6. Add the remaining ingredients.

Simple Breakfast Sausages

Serving size: 6

Preparation time: 5 minutes

Cooking time: 15 minutes

Ingredients:

- 6 pork sausages, pricked with a sharp knife
- ½ cup onions
- ½ cup red wine
- ½ cup water
- Salt and pepper to taste

Instruction:

1. Place all ingredients in the Power Pressure Cooker XL.
2. Close the lid and press the Meat/Chicken button and cook on preset cooking time.
3. Release the steam.
4. Serve with potato mash.

Rustic Oat Carrot Cake

Serving size: 4

Preparation time: 10 minutes

Cooking time: 10 minutes

Ingredients:

- 1 cup steel cut oats
- 1 ½ cups milk
- 1 cup carrots, shredded
- ½ cup sugar
- ½ teaspoon cinnamon

Instruction:

1. Combine all ingredients in a heat-proof bowl or baking pan. Cover the pan with aluminum foil. Set aside.
2. Place a steamer rack inside the Power Pressure Cooker XL.
3. Place the baking pan on the steamer rack.
4. Add 1 cup water in the inner pot.
5. Close the lid and press the Fish/Vegetable/Steam button.

6. Adjust the timer to 10 minutes.

7. Let the pressure cooker release steam naturally.

8. Serve warm.

Sweet Rice Pudding

Serving size: 2

Preparation time: 5 minutes

Cooking time: 11 minutes

Ingredients:
- 1 cup Arborio rice
- 2 cups whole milk, divided
- 1 cup raisin
- 2 eggs
- ½ teaspoon vanilla

Instruction:
1. Mix the rice, half of the milk, and raisins in the Power Pressure Cooker XL.
2. Close the lid and press the Rice button.
3. Once the timer sets off, release the pressure naturally.
4. Open the lid and press the Rice button once more.
5. Add the remaining milk and the eggs. Stir constantly to incorporate the mixture.
6. Cook for another 5 minutes while stirring constantly.
7. Serve warm.

Cheesy Pressure Cooker Egg "Bake"

Serving size: 4

Preparation time: 10 minutes

Cooking time: 10 minutes

Ingredients:

- 6 slices of bacon, chopped finely
- 6 eggs
- ¼ cup milk
- ½ cup shredded cheddar cheese
- 1 cup mashed potato

Instruction:

1. In a baking dish, mix all ingredients together. Cover with foil and set aside.
2. Place a steamer rack in the Power Pressure Cooker XL.
3. Add 1 cup of water in the inner pot.
4. Place the baking dish on the steamer rack.
5. Close the lid.
6. Press the Fish/Vegetable/Steam button and cook on default setting.
7. Do natural pressure release for 10-minutes.

Easy Breakfast Raisin Oats

Serving size: 2

Preparation time: 5 minutes

Cooking time: 10 minutes

Ingredients:

- 1 tablespoon butter
- 1 cup steel cut oats
- 3 ½ cups water
- ¼ teaspoon salt
- ¾ cup raisins

Instruction:

1. Press the Rice/Risotto button on the Power Pressure Cooker XL.
2. Add the butter and melt. Add in the oats and toast while stirring constantly until they darken.
3. Add the water, salt, and raisins.
4. Close the lid and adjust the cooking time to 10 minutes.
5. Let the pressure release naturally.
6. Serve warm.

Gluten-Fee Banana Bread

Serving size: 10

Preparation time: 10 minutes

Cooking time: 10 minutes

Ingredients:

- 3 medium ripe bananas
- 2 cups old-fashioned rolled oats
- ¼ cup maple syrup
- 2 large eggs
- 1 teaspoon baking soda

Instruction:

1. Combine all ingredients in a bowl.
2. Pour the mixture in a baking pan that can fit inside the Power Pressure Cooker XL. Cover the top with aluminum foil.
3. Place a steamer rack in the pressure cooker and add 1 cup of water to generate pressure.
4. Place the baking pan on the steamer rack.
5. Close the lid and press the Fish/Vegetable/Steam button. Adjust the timer to 10 minutes.
6. Let the steam release naturally.
7. Let it cool before serving.

Breakfast Stuffed Sweet Potatoes

Serving size: 2

Preparation time: 5 minutes

Cooking time: 13 minutes

Ingredients:

- 1 medium sweet potato
- 2 slices bacon, chopped
- 2 large eggs
- Salt and pepper to taste
- ¼ cup cheese, shredded

Instruction:

1. Wash the sweet potato and pierce with a fork.
2. Place inside the Power Pressure Cooker XL and add 1 cup water.
3. Close the lid and press the Fish/Vegetable/Steam button.
4. Adjust the cooking time to 10 minutes.
5. Release the pressure and take out the sweet potato.
6. Let it cool then cut lengthwise.
7. Without the lid on, press the Meat/Chicken button

and cook the bacon. Set aside.

8. Add the eggs and scramble for 3 minutes. Season with salt and pepper to taste.

9. Assemble the sweet potato by mashing the center with a fork. Top with bacon, scrambled egg, and cheese.

Healthy Vegetarian Frittata

Serving size: 4

Preparation time: 5 minutes

Cooking time: 4 minutes

Ingredients:

- 4 large eggs
- ½ cup cheddar cheese, shredded
- 1 medium tomato, chopped
- 1 tablespoon chives, chopped
- ½ green bell pepper, chopped

Instruction:

1. Mix all ingredients in a mixing bowl.
2. Pour in a heat-proof dish that can fit in the Power Pressure Cooker XL. Cover with aluminum foil.
3. Place a steamer rack in the pressure cooker and add 1 cup of water.
4. Place the dish with the egg mixture.
5. Close the lid.
6. Select the Fish/Vegetable/Steam button and cook for 4 minutes.
7. Let the pressure release naturally.

Quinoa Power Breakfast Bowl

Serving size: 1

Preparation time: 3 minutes

Cooking time: 6 minutes

Ingredients:

- ½ cup quinoa
- ½ banana, sliced
- 1/3 cup blueberries
- 1/3 cup almond milk
- 1 tablespoon peanut butter

Instruction:

1. Place the quinoa in the Power Pressure Cooker XL. Pour 2 ½ cups of water.
2. Close the lid and press the Rice/Risotto button. Cook on preset cooking time.
3. Release the pressure naturally.
4. Let it cool before assembling.
5. Top the quinoa with the rest of the ingredients.
6. Serve chilled.

Steamed Ham and Swiss Omelet

Serving size: 4

Preparation time: 5 minutes

Cooking time: 10 minutes

Ingredients:

- 3 eggs
- 1 tablespoon butter
- Salt and pepper to taste
- ½ cup ham, cubed
- ¼ cup Swiss cheese, shredded

Instruction:

1. Mix all ingredients and place in a heat-proof dish that can fit in your Power Pressure Cooker XL. Cover with aluminum foil.
2. Place a steamer rack in the pressure cooker and pour 1 cup water.
3. Close the lid.
4. Press the Fish/Vegetable/Steam button and adjust the timer for 10 minutes.
5. Release the pressure naturally.

Healthy Herb and Onion Frittata

Serving size: 1

Preparation time: 5 minutes

Cooking time: 10 minutes

Ingredients:

- 1 cup onion, diced
- ¼ cup water
- 3 eggs
- 2 teaspoon fresh herbs of your choice
- 2 tablespoon ricotta cheese, shredded

Instruction:

1. Mix all ingredients in a mixing bowl.
2. Pour in a heat-proof dish that will fit the Power Pressure Cooker XL.
3. Cover with aluminum foil.
4. Place a steamer rack in the pressure cooker and pour 1 cup water.
5. Place the dish with the egg mixture.
6. Close the lid.
7. Press the Fish/Vegetable/Steam and cook for 10 minutes.
8. Let the pressure release naturally.

Rustic Yankee Grits

Serving size: 1

Preparation time: 5 minutes

Cooking time: 10 minutes

Ingredients:

- 1 cup low fat milk
- A pinch of salt
- 2 teaspoon maple syrup
- ¼ up cooking grits
- 2 tablespoon raisins

Instruction:

1. Press the Rice/Risotto button while the lid is not yet closed.
2. Pour the milk and bring to a boil.
3. Add the salt and maple syrup.
4. Mix in the grits and raisins.
5. Close the lid and adjust the timer to 10 minutes.
6. Let the pressure release naturally.

Fast And Easy Rice Porridge

Serving size: 2

Preparation time: 5 minutes

Cooking time: 6 minutes

Ingredients:

- 1 cup rolled oats
- ½ cup milk
- ½ cup brown sugar
- ½ cup yogurt

Instruction:

1. Place all ingredients in the Power Pressure Cooker XL.
2. Give it a good mix to incorporate all ingredients.
3. Close the lid.
4. Press the Rice/Risotto button and cook under preset cooking time.
5. Let the pressure release naturally.

Lunch Recipes

Soup and Rice Recipes

Beefy Corn and Black Chili Soup

Serving size: 6

Preparation time: 5 minutes

Cooking time: 15 minutes

Ingredients:
- 1 pound ground beef
- 1 teaspoon chili powder
- 1 can black beans, drained
- 1 ½ cup beef broth
- 1 can tomatoes

Instruction:
1. Pour all ingredients in the Power Pressure Cooker XL.
2. Close the lid and press the Soup/Stew button.
3. Cook for 15 minutes.
4. Let the pressure release naturally.

Easy Pressure Cooker Posole

Serving size: 6

Preparation time: 5 minutes

Cooking time: 20 minutes

Ingredients:

- 1 small package chipotle seasoning blend
- 1 can white hominy or corn grits
- 1 can stewed tomatoes
- Fresh cilantro
- 1 pound tenderloin

Instruction:

1. Mix all ingredients in the Power Pressure Cooker.
2. Give it a good stir to incorporate all ingredients.
3. Close the lid and press the Soup/Stew button.
4. Adjust the timer and cook for 20 minutes.
5. Let the pressure release immediately.

Spicy Poblano And Corn Soup

Serving size: 4

Preparation time: 5 minutes

Cooking time: 10 minutes

Ingredients:

- 1 cup fat-free milk
- 1 package frozen baby corn
- 4 poblano or green chilies
- 1 onion, chopped
- ¼ cup cheddar cheese

Instruction:

1. Combine all ingredients except the cheddar cheese in the Power Pressure Cooker XL.
2. Close the lid and press the Soup/Stew button.
3. Cook for 5 minutes.
4. Release the pressure quickly to open the lid.
5. Without the lid, press the Soup/Stew button again and set it for 5 minutes.
6. Add the cheese and cook until the soup thickens slightly.

Creamy Sweet Potato, Leek and Ham Soup

Serving size: 4

Preparation time: 5 minutes

Cooking time: 13 minutes

Ingredients:

- 1 cup ham, diced
- 1 leek, chopped
- 1 large sweet potato, chopped
- 2 cups chicken broth
- 1 cup evaporated milk

Instruction:

1. Press the Soup/Stew button on the Power Pressure Cooker XL.
2. Add the ham and sauté to render some of its fat. Stir in the leeks and sweet potatoes. Cook for another 3 minutes.
3. Pour in the broth and milk.
4. Close and lock the lid.
5. Adjust the cooking time to 10 minutes.
6. Let the pressure release naturally.

Delightful Chicken and White Bean Soup

Serving size: 4

Preparation time: 5 minutes

Cooking time: 5 minutes

Ingredients:

- 2 cups chicken breast, boneless and shredded
- 1 tablespoon taco seasoning
- 2 cans chicken broth
- 1 can cannellini beans, soaked

Instruction:

1. Place all ingredients in the Power Pressure Cooker XL.
2. Close the lid and press the Soup/Stew button. Cook on preset cooking time.
3. Let the pressure release naturally.
4. Garnish with cilantro, light sour cream or green salsa if desired.

Flavorful Vegetarian Bean Soup

Serving size: 4

Preparation time: 5 minutes

Cooking time: 6 minutes

Ingredients:

- 1 can vegetable broth
- 1 can refried beans
- 1 can black beans, drained
- 2 cups frozen corn
- 1 can tomatoes and chilies

Instruction:

1. Mix all ingredients in the Power Pressure Cooker XL.
2. Give a good stir to incorporate all ingredients.
3. Close the lid and press the Bean/Lentil button.
4. Let the steam release naturally.
5. Serve warm.

Pressure Cooker Classic Wild Rice

Serving size: 6

Preparation time: 5 minutes

Cooking time: 35 minutes

Ingredients:

- 2 cups wild rice
- 3 cups water
- 3 cups bone broth
- 2 teaspoon salt

Instruction:

1. Add all ingredients in the Power Pressure Cooker XL.
2. Place the lid on and lock it into place.
3. Press the Rice/Risotto button and adjust the cooking time to 35 minutes.
4. Once you hear the beep, let the pressure release naturally.
5. Serve with soup or mixed vegetables.

Spicy Chili Rice Casserole

Serving size: 8

Preparation time: 10 minutes

Cooking time: 20 minutes

Ingredients:

- 3 cups white rice
- 5 cups water
- 2 eggs beaten
- 1 can chopped green chilies
- 2 cups Monterey Jack cheese, shredded

Instruction:

1. Place the rice and water in the Power Pressure Cooker XL.
2. Close the lid and lock it into place.
3. Press the Rice/Risotto setting and cook adjust the timer to 15 minutes.
4. Let the pressure release naturally once cooked.
5. Open the lid and fluff the rice with fork.
6. Press the Rice/Risotto setting while the pot is open.
7. Stir in the eggs, green chilies and cheese until well

combined.

8. Cook while the lid is open for 5 minutes or until the eggs are done.

No Brainer Basmati Rice

Serving size: 3

Preparation time: 5minutes

Cooking time: 15 minutes

Ingredients:

- 1 ½ cups basmati rice
- 3 cups water
- Salt and pepper to taste
- 1 lemon, juiced
- 1 cup fresh basil leaves, chopped

Instruction:

1. Mix all ingredients in the Power Pressure Cooker XL.
2. Close the lid and lock it in place.
3. Press the Rice/Risotto button and adjust the cooking time to 15 minutes.
4. Release the pressure naturally once the pressure cooker beeps.

Savory Rice Chicken Porridge

Serving size: 6

Preparation time: 5 minutes

Cooking time: 20 minutes

Ingredients:

- 4-pound chicken, cut into chunks
- 10 cups water
- 1 cup long grain rice
- 1 3-inch long ginger, sliced
- Salt to taste

Instruction:

1. Place all ingredients in the Power Pressure Cooker XL.
2. Close the lid and lock it into place.
3. Press the Rice/Risotto button.
4. Adjust the cooking time to 20 minutes.
5. Once the pressure cooker beeps, let the pressure release naturally.
6. Serve with scallions or a tablespoon of sesame oil.

Sweet And Creamy Rice Porridge

Serving size: 3

Preparation time: 5 minutes

Cooking time: 12 minutes

Ingredients:

- 2 ½ cups milk
- 1 egg yolk
- 1 cup uncooked rice
- 1 teaspoon vanilla extract
- ¼ cup white sugar

Instruction:

1. In a bowl, mix together the milk and egg. Set aside.
2. Press the Rice/Risotto button on the Power Pressure Cooker XL.
3. Add the rice and toast it for 2 minutes.
4. Pour in the milk mixture and the rest of the ingredients. Stir to combine.
5. Close the lid.
6. Adjust the cooking time to 10 minutes.
7. Let the pressure release naturally.

Chicken Recipes

Superb Pressure Cooker Chicken Manicotti

Serving size: 7

Preparation time: 10 minutes

Cooking time: 15 minutes

Ingredients:

- 1 ½ pound chicken, boneless and skin removed
- 1 teaspoon Italian seasoning
- 14 uncooked manicotti shells
- 2 cups spaghetti sauce
- 2 cups mozzarella cheese, shredded

Instruction:

1. Season the chicken with Italian seasoning. Set aside.
2. Place the manicotti shells on the bottom of the Power pressure cooker.
3. Pour the seasoned chicken on top of the manicotti shells.

4. Add the spaghetti sauce and top with mozzarella cheese.
5. Close the lid and press the Rice/Risotto button.
6. Adjust the cooking time to 15 minutes.
7. Once you hear the beep, let the pressure release naturally.

Flavorful Chicken Tortellini

Serving size: 6

Preparation time: 10 minutes

Cooking time: 15 minutes

Ingredients:

- 1 package tortellini
- 2 cups broccoli, sliced into florets
- 1 ½ cup packaged Alfredo sauce
- 2 cups chicken breast, cut into strips
- 1/3 cup soft bread crumbs

Instruction:

1. In the Power Pressure Cooker XL, mix together the pasta, broccoli, Alfredo sauce, and chicken. Mix until well combined.
2. Add in the bread crumbs on top.
3. Close the lid of the pressure cooker.
4. Press the Meat/Chicken button and cook on preset time.
5. Let the pressure release naturally.

One Pot Sweet and Spicy Chicken

Serving size: 6

Preparation time: 5 minutes

Cooking time: 20 minutes

Ingredients:

- 2 pounds' chicken, bones and skin removed
- 3 cloves of garlic, minced
- 1 cup packaged sweet and sour sauce
- ¾ cup packaged barbecue sauce
- 2 tablespoon cornstarch + 2 tablespoon water

Instruction:

1. Place the first four ingredients in the Power Pressure Cooker.
2. Stir to combine.
3. Close the lid and press the Meat/Chicken button. Cook for 15 minutes.
4. Once it beeps, release the pressure naturally.
5. Open the lid and press the Meat/Chicken button.
6. Add the cornstarch slurry and mix until the sauce thickens.

7. Press the Cancel button to stop the cooking process.

8. Serve warm.

Savory Honey Chicken

Serving size: 8

Preparation time: 5 minutes

Cooking time: 15 minutes

Ingredients:

- 8 chicken thighs
- ½ teaspoon ginger, ground
- Salt and pepper to taste
- ½ cup honey
- ½ cup water

Instruction:

1. Place all ingredients in the Power Pressure Cooker XL.
2. Close the lid and press the Meat/Chicken button.
3. Once it beeps, release the pressure to open the lid.
4. Serve with egg noodles and sesame seeds.

Cream Italian Chicken

Serving size: 6

Preparation time: 5 minutes

Cooking time: 15 minutes

Ingredients:

- 1 pound chicken breast, bones and skin removed
- 1 block cream cheese, softened
- 1 7-ounce package Italian dressing mix
- ½ cup water
- Pepper to taste

Instruction:

1. Place all ingredients in the Power Pressure Cooker XL.
2. Stir to combine.
3. Close the lid and press the Meat/Chicken button.
4. Once the pressure cooker beeps, release the pressure to open the lid.

Peanut Chicken

Serving size: 12

Preparation time: 5 minutes

Cooking time: 15 minutes

Ingredients:

- 3-pounds chicken breast, bones and skin removed
- ½ cup chunky peanut butter
- ½ cup orange juice
- 1 cup chicken broth
- Salt and pepper to taste

Instruction:

1. Place all ingredients in the Power Pressure Cooker XL.
2. Close the lid and press the Meat/Chicken button.
3. Cook on preset cooking time.
4. Do quick pressure release.

Creamy Chicken Supreme

Serving size: 6

Preparation time: 10 minutes

Cooking time: 25 minutes

Ingredients:

- 5 slices of bacon
- 6 boneless chicken breast, halved
- 1 cup mushroom, sliced
- 1 can condensed cream of chicken soup
- ½ cup Swiss cheese, diced

Instruction:

1. Press the Meat/Chicken button on the Power Pressure Cooker XL.
2. Place the bacon and stir until crispy and the oil has rendered. Crumble the crispy bacon. Set aside.
3. Add the chicken and stir until slightly browned.
4. Add in the mushroom and chicken soup.
5. Close the lid and adjust the cooking time to 20 minutes.
6. Do quick pressure release once the pressure cooker

beeps.

7. Press the Meat/Chicken button again and add the cheese. Stir until well combined and the cheese has slightly melted.

8. Add in the bacon bits.

Savory Santa Fe Chicken

Serving size: 6

Preparation time: 5 minutes

Cooking time: 15 minutes

Ingredients:

- 1 can black beans, drained and rinsed
- 2 cans whole kernel corns, drained
- 6 boneless chicken breast, skin removed
- 1 cup packaged salsa
- 1 cup cheddar cheese, shredded

Instruction:

1. Mix all the ingredients in the Power Pressure Cooker XL.
2. Close the lid and press the Meat/Chicken button.
3. Cook on preset cooking time.
4. Do quick pressure release.
5. Serve with tortilla, sour cream, and cilantro if desired.

Sweet And Tangy Cola Chicken

Serving size: 12

Preparation time: 5 minutes

Cooking time: 15 minutes

Ingredients:

- 1 onion, peeled and chopped
- 1 frying chicken, cut into smaller parts
- Salt and pepper to taste
- 1 cup ketchup
- 1 cup Dr. Pepper or cola

Instruction:

1. Place the onions at the bottom of the inner pot.
2. Add the chicken pieces on top and sprinkle with salt and pepper.
3. Add ketchup and cola.
4. Close the lid and press the Meat/Chicken button.
5. Cook on preset cooking time.
6. Do quick pressure release.

Juicy And Tender Pulled Chicken

Serving size: 6

Preparation time: 5 minutes

Cooking time: 43 minutes

Ingredients:

- 1 pound chicken breast
- 1 cup onion, chopped
- 1 ½ cup tomato ketchup
- 2 tablespoon Worcestershire sauce
- Salt and pepper to taste

Instruction:

1. Press the Meat/Chicken button on the Power Pressure Cooker XL.
2. Add the chicken pieces and brown for 3 minutes on each side.
3. Pour the rest of the ingredients.
4. Close the lid and adjust the cooking time to 40 minutes.
5. Do quick pressure release to remove the chicken pieces.

6. Press the Meat/Chicken button and continue to cook the sauce until it slightly thickens

7. Use a fork to shred the chicken meat.

8. Place the shredded chicken meat in the pot and stir to coat the sauce.

Beef Recipes

Java-Infused Roast Beef

Serving size: 12

Preparation time: 5 minutes

Cooking time: 40 minutes

Ingredients:

- 3-pounds boneless beef chuck roast
- 5 cloves of garlic, crushed
- salt and pepper to taste
- 1 cup strong brewed coffee
- 2 tablespoon cornstarch + water

Instruction:

1. Add the first four ingredients in the Power Pressure Cooker XL.
2. Close the lid and press the Meat/Chicken button.
3. Adjust the cooking time and cook for 40 minutes.
4. Release the pressure to open the lid.
5. Press the Meat/Chicken button once the lid is open

and add the cornstarch slurry.

6. Cook for five minutes until the sauce thickens.

7. Press the Cancel button.

Creamy Enchilada Casserole

Serving size: 6

Preparation time: 10 minutes

Cooking time: 30 minutes

Ingredients:

- 1 pound ground beef
- 2 cans enchilada sauce
- 1 can cream of onion soup
- 1 packaged flour tortillas, torn
- 3 cups cheddar cheese, shredded

Instruction:

1. Press the Meat/Chicken button and add the ground beef. Stir constantly for 3 minutes until it has browned.
2. Add the enchilada sauce and onion soup.
3. Close the lid and adjust the cooking time to 25 minutes.
4. Do quick pressure release to open the lid.
5. Press the Meat/Chicken button again and add the tortilla chips and cheese.

6. Stir to combine and cook without the lid on for 5 minutes.

7. Press the Cancel/Keep Warm button.

Flavorsome Tomato Hamburger Soup

Serving size: 12

Preparation time: 5 minutes

Cooking time: 20 minutes

Ingredients:

- 1 can V8 juice
- 1 pound ground beef
- 2 packages frozen mixed vegetables
- 1 can cream of mushroom soup
- Salt and pepper to taste

Instruction:

1. Place all ingredients in the Power Pressure Cooker XL.
2. Close the lid and press the Meat/Chicken button.
3. Adjust the cooking time for 20 minutes.
4. Once the pressure cooker beeps, release the pressure immediately.
5. Serve warm.

Gourmet Pressure Cooker Italian Beef

Serving size: 6

Preparation time: 5 minutes

Cooking time: 40 minutes

Ingredients:

- Pound chuck roast, fat trimmed and cut into chunks
- 1 package Italian salad dressing mix
- 8 ounce pepperoncini pepper, sliced
- 3 cups beef broth
- Provolone cheese slices for garnish

Instruction:

1. Place all ingredients except for the cheese slices inside the Power Pressure Cooker.
2. Close the lid and select the Meat/Chicken button.
3. Adjust the cooking time to 40 minutes.
4. Once the pressure cooker beeps, do quick pressure release.
5. Serve the beef with cheese slices on top and in a bun.

Steak Pizzaiola

Serving size: 4

Preparation time: 5 minutes

Cooking time: 40 minutes

Ingredients:

- 2-pounds beef roast, cut into chunks
- 1 medium onion, sliced
- 1 yellow sweet bell pepper, sliced
- 1 jar pasta sauce
- ¼ cup water

Instruction:

1. Place all ingredients inside the Power Pressure Cooker XL.
2. Close the lid and press the Meat/Chicken button.
3. Adjust the cooking time for 40 minutes.
4. Release the pressure naturally.
5. Serve warm.

No-Frill Swiss Steak

Serving size: 6

Preparation time: 5 minutes

Cooking time: 40 minutes

Ingredients:

- 1 ½ pound beef round steak, cut into piece
- Salt and pepper to taste
- 1 onion, sliced
- 1 rib of celery, sliced
- 2 cans tomato sauce

Instruction:

1. Put all ingredients in the Power Pressure Cooker XL.
2. Close the lid and press the Meat/Chicken button.
3. Adjust the cooking time to 40 minutes.
4. Release the pressure naturally.

Glazed Brisket with Cranberry Gravy

Serving size: 8

Preparation time: 5 minutes

Cooking time: 40 minutes

Ingredients:

- 2-pounds beef brisket, sliced
- Salt and pepper to taste
- 1 can cranberry sauce
- 1 can tomato sauce
- ½ cup onion, chopped

Instruction:

1. Put all ingredients in the Power Pressure Cooker XL.
2. Close the lid and press the Meat/Chicken button.
3. Adjust the cooking time to 40 minutes.
4. Release the pressure naturally.

Asian-Inspired Sesame Beef

Serving size: 6

Preparation time: 10 minutes

Cooking time: 45 minutes

Ingredients:

- 1 ½ pounds rump beef, sliced
- 3 tablespoon soy sauce
- 2 cups beef broth
- ¼ cup sesame seeds
- 2 tablespoon cornstarch + 2 tablespoon water

Instruction:

1. Place all ingredients except the sesame seeds and cornstarch slurry in the Power Pressure Cooker XL.
2. Close the lid and press the Meat/Chicken button.
3. Cook for 40 minutes by adjusting the cooking timer.
4. Once it beeps, release the pressure.
5. Press the Meat/Chicken button again and add the cornstarch slurry.
6. Stir until the sauce thickens.
7. Press the cancel button to turn off the pressure cooker.
8. Sprinkle with sesame seeds.

Pork Recipes

Cherrific Balsamic Pork Loin

Serving size: 8

Preparation time: 5 minutes

Cooking time: 5 minutes

Ingredients:

- 3-pounds boneless pork loin roast
- Salt and pepper to taste
- ¾ cup cherry preserves
- 1/3 cup balsamic vinegar
- ½ cup dried cherries

Instruction:

1. Place all ingredients in the Power Pressure Cooker XL.
2. Close the lid and press the Meat/Chicken button.
3. Adjust the cooking timer to 40 minutes.
4. Once the pressure cooker beeps, do quick pressure release to open the lid.

Sweet And Sour Pineapple Barbecue Sauce Pork Chops

Serving size: 4

Preparation time: 5 minutes

Cooking time: 40 minutes

Ingredients:

- 4 bone in pork loin chops
- 1 can crushed pineapples, undrained
- 1/3 cup onion, chopped
- 1 cup honey barbecue sauce
- 2 tablespoon chili sauce

Instruction:

1. Mix all ingredients in the Power Pressure Cooker XL.
2. Close the lid and press the Meat/Chicken button.
3. Adjust the cooking timer to 40 minutes.
4. Once the pressure cooker beeps, do quick pressure release to open the lid.
5. Serve with rice or salad.

Not-Your-Ordinary Pork and Beans

Serving size: 12

Preparation time: 5 minutes

Cooking time: 40 minutes

Ingredients:

- 3-pounds pork tenderloin, cut into thin strips
- 2 cans black beans, rinsed and drained
- 1 jar picante sauce
- Salt and pepper to taste

Instruction:

1. Mix all ingredients in the Power Pressure Cooker XL.
2. Close the lid and press the Meat/Chicken button.
3. Adjust the cooking timer to 40 minutes.
4. Once the pressure cooker beeps, do quick pressure release to open the lid.

Effortless Dr. Pepper Pulled Pork

Serving size: 6

Preparation time: 5 minutes

Cooking time: 60 minutes

Ingredients:

- 3-pounds pork loin roast
- 1 envelope of your favorite seasoning
- 2 cans Dr. Pepper or cola of your choice
- 1 can barbecue sauce

Instruction:

1. Mix all ingredients in the Power Pressure Cooker XL.
2. Close the lid and press the Meat/Chicken button.
3. Adjust the cooking timer to 60 minutes.
4. Once the pressure cooker beeps, do quick pressure release to open the lid.
5. Take the pork out and shred using fork.
6. Place the shredded meat back and press the Meat/Chicken button.
7. Cook until the sauce thickens

Saucy Ranch Pork and Potatoes

Serving size: 6

Preparation time: 5 minutes

Cooking time: 40 minutes

Ingredients:

- 2 pounds red potatoes, cubed
- ¼ cup water
- 6 pork loin chops
- 1 envelope ranch salad dressing mix
- 2 cans cream of chicken soup

Instruction:

1. Mix all ingredients in the Power Pressure Cooker XL.
2. Close the lid and press the Meat/Chicken button.
3. Adjust the cooking timer to 40 minutes.
4. Once the pressure cooker beeps, do quick pressure release to open the lid.

Dinner Recipes

Pork and Fish Recipes

Delish Caribbean Pork Roast

Serving size: 6

Preparation time: 5 minutes

Cooking time: 40 minutes

Ingredients:

- 4-pounds pork loin roast
- 1 cup apple juice
- 1 tablespoon curry powder
- 1 teaspoon cumin
- Salt and pepper to taste

Instruction:

1. Place all ingredients inside the Power Pressure Cooker XL.
2. Stir to combine everything.
3. Close the lid and press the Meat/Chicken button.

4. Adjust the cooking timer to 40 minutes.

5. Once the pressure cooker beeps, do quick pressure release to open the lid.

6. Press the Meat/Chicken button and let it cook without the lid until the sauce slightly thickens.

7. Press the Cancel/Keep Warm button to turn it off.

Easy-Breezy Orange Pork Roast

Serving size: 12

Preparation time: 5 minutes

Cooking time: 45 minutes

Ingredients:

- 3-pounds pork shoulder roast
- 1 can frozen orange juice, concentrated
- Salt and pepper to taste
- 2 tablespoon flour + 2 tablespoon water

Instruction:

1. Place all ingredients in the Power Pressure Cooker XL except for the last ingredient. This will be the thickener.
2. Close the lid and press the Meat/Chicken button.
3. Adjust the cooking timer to 40 minutes.
4. Once the pressure cooker beeps, do quick pressure release to open the lid.
5. Press the Meat/Chicken button and let it cook without the lid until the sauce slightly thickens.
6. Press the Cancel/Keep Warm button to turn it off.

One-Pot Honey Mustard Pork

Serving size: 6

Preparation time: 5 minutes

Cooking time: 1 hour and 5 minutes

Ingredients:

- 3-pounds boneless pork roast
- ¾ cup chicken broth
- 1/3 cup honey mustard
- Salt and pepper to taste
- 2 tablespoon cornstarch + 2 tablespoon water

Instruction:

1. Place all ingredients in the Power Pressure Cooker XL except for cornstarch slurry.
2. Close the lid and press the Meat/Chicken button.
3. Adjust the cooking timer to 60 minutes.
4. Once the pressure cooker beeps, do quick pressure release to open the lid.
5. Press the Meat/Chicken button and let it cook without the lid until the sauce slightly thickens.
6. Press the Cancel/Keep Warm button to turn it off.

Peppery Pork Chops

Serving size: 6

Preparation time: 5 minutes

Cooking time: 30 minutes

Ingredients:

- 4-pieces thick pork loin chops
- Salt and pepper to taste
- 3 tablespoon white wine Worcestershire sauce
- 2 red bell peppers, seeded and cut into strips
- ½ cup chicken broth

Instruction:

1. Place all ingredients in the Power Pressure Cooker XL.
2. Close the lid and press the Meat/Chicken button.
3. Adjust the cooking timer to 30 minutes.
4. Once the pressure cooker beeps, do quick pressure release to open the lid.

Salmon with Caramelized Onions and Carrots

Serving size: 3

Preparation time: 5 minutes

Cooking time: 21 minutes

Ingredients:

- 1 ½ pounds salmon fillet
- Salt and pepper to taste
- 2 tablespoon butter
- 4 onions, chopped
- 1 bag baby carrots, rinsed

Instruction:

1. Season the salmon with salt and pepper. Place in a dish that will fit in the Power Pressure Cooker XL. Set aside.
2. Press the Fish/Vegetable/Steam button on the Power Pressure Cooker and adjust the time to 15 minutes.
3. Melt the butter and add the onions. Constantly stir

until the onions become caramelized. Set aside.

4. Add the baby carrots and cook for 2 minutes.

5. Place the carrots on top of the salmon.

6. Place a steamer rack in the pressure cooker and add 1 cup of water.

7. Place the baking dish with the salmon and carrots.

8. Close the lid and adjust the timer to 6 minutes.

9. Do quick pressure release.

10. Top with caramelized onions.

Easy-To-Cook Honey Orange Fish Fillet

Serving size: 4

Preparation time: 10 minutes

Cooking time: 10 minutes

Ingredients:

- 1 ½ pounds fish fillet of your choice
- Salt and pepper to taste
- 3 tablespoon frozen orange juice concentrate
- 2 tablespoon honey
- ½ teaspoon dried dill weed

Instruction:

1. Season the fish fillet with salt and pepper.
2. Place in a ramekin or dish that can fit inside the Power Pressure Cooker XL.
3. Pour over the orange juice and honey. Massage the fish gently.
4. Sprinkle with honey and dill weed.
5. Place a steamer rack in the pressure cooker and place the dish on top.
6. Pour 1 cup water in the pot.

7. Close the lid and press the Fish/Vegetable/Steam button.

8. Adjust the cooking time to 10 minutes.

9. Do quick pressure release.

Creamy Fish Chowder

Serving size: 6

Preparation time: 5 minutes

Cooking time: 10 minutes

Ingredients:

- 2-pounds frozen fish fillet
- 1 can evaporated milk diluted with 2 cups water
- Salt and pepper to taste
- 1 onion, chopped
- 4 red potatoes, chopped

Instruction:

1. Place all ingredients in the Power Pressure Cooker XL.
2. Close the lid and press the Fish/Vegetable/Steam button.
3. Adjust the cooking timer to 10 minutes.
4. Once the pressure cooker beeps, do quick pressure release to open the lid.

Not-So-Fishy Fish Fillet with Mushroom Sauce

Serving size: 6
Preparation time: 5 minutes
Cooking time: 10 minutes

Ingredients:

- 1 ½ pounds fish fillet (any white fish)
- 1 ½ cups cremini mushrooms, sliced
- 1 cup milk
- Salt and pepper to taste
- 2 tablespoon lemon juice

Instruction:

1. Place all ingredients in the Power Pressure Cooker XL.
2. Close the lid and press the Fish/Vegetable/Steam button.
3. Adjust the cooking timer to 10 minutes.
4. Once the pressure cooker beeps, do quick pressure release to open the lid.

Beef Recipes

Home-Style Beef Stew

Serving size: 5
Preparation time: 5 minutes
Cooking time: 25 minutes

Ingredients:
- 1 package frozen vegetables of your choice
- 1 ½ pounds beef stew meat, cut into cubes
- 1 can tomato soup
- 1 can cream of mushroom soup
- 2 tablespoon onion powder

Instruction:
1. Place all ingredients in the Power Pressure Cooker XL.
2. Close the lid and press the Meat/Chicken button.
3. Adjust the cooking timer to 25 minutes.
4. Once the pressure cooker beeps, do quick pressure release to open the lid.

Spicy Chili Colorado Burritos

Serving size: 8

Preparation time: 5 minutes

Cooking time: 45 minutes

Ingredients:

- 2-pounds boneless beef chuck roast
- 2 cans enchilada sauce
- 8 flour tortillas
- 1 cup Monterey Jack cheese, shredded
- A sprig of green onions, chopped

Instruction:

1. Place the beef chuck roast and enchilada sauce in the Power Pressure Cooker XL.
2. Close the lid and press the Meat/Chicken button.
3. Adjust the cooking timer to 40 minutes.
4. Once the pressure cooker beeps, do quick pressure release to open the lid.
5. Get the chuck roast out from the pressure cooker and transfer it to a bowl.
6. Shred the meat using fork.
7. Place the shredded meat back to the pressure cooker.

8. Press the Meat/Chicken button and cook without the lid on for 5 minutes or until the sauce thickens.

9. Assemble the burritos by placing the shredded meat into the tortillas topped with cheese and onions.

No-Sweat Skirt Steak with Vegetables

Serving size: 2

Preparation time: 5 minutes

Cooking time: 15 minutes

Ingredients:

- 1 pound skirt steak, sliced into strips
- 2 cups mixed vegetables like peas and corn
- 1 cup water
- Salt and pepper to taste
- A sprig of fresh thyme

Instruction:

1. Place all ingredients in the Power Pressure Cooker XL.
2. Close the lid and press the Meat/Chicken button.
3. Adjust the cooking timer to 15 minutes.
4. Once the pressure cooker beeps, do quick pressure release to open the lid.

Gourmet Pressure Cooker Beef Tenderloin Steak with Red Wine Mushroom Sauce

Serving size: 4
Preparation time: 5 minutes
Cooking time: 28 minutes

Ingredients:

- 2 tablespoon butter
- 1 ½ pounds beef tenderloin steak, trimmed from fat
- Salt and pepper to taste
- 1 pack Portobello mushrooms, sliced
- 1 cup dry red wine

Instruction:

1. Press the Meat/Chicken button on the Power Pressure Cooker XL.
2. Heat the butter and add the steak. Season with salt and pepper.
3. Sear and slightly brown each side for 3 minutes.
4. Mix in the mushrooms and red wine.

5. Close the lid and adjust the cooking time to 25 minutes.
6. Do quick pressure release to open the lid.
7. If the sauce has not thickened enough, continue cooking without the lid on.

Homemade Beef Pot Roast

Serving size: 8

Preparation time: 5 minutes

Cooking time: 45 minutes

Ingredients:

- ¼ cup water
- ¼ cup ketchup
- 1 tablespoon Worcestershire sauce
- Salt and pepper to taste
- 2-pounds boneless beef pot roast

Instruction:

1. Place all ingredients in the Power Pressure Cooker XL.
2. Close the lid and press the Meat/Chicken button.
3. Adjust the cooking timer to 40 minutes.
4. Once the pressure cooker beeps, do quick pressure release to open the lid.
5. Press the Meat/Chicken button again and cook without the lid on to reduce the sauce.

Pressure Cooker Beef Stroganoff

Serving size: 4

Preparation time: 5 minutes

Cooking time: 50 minutes

Ingredients:

- 1 pound stew meat
- 1 can cream of mushroom soup
- 1 can cream of onion soup
- 8-ounces egg noodles
- ½ cup sour cream

Instruction:

1. Place the meat, cream of mushroom soup, and cream of onion soup in the Power Pressure Cooker XL.
2. Close the lid and press the Meat/Chicken button.
3. Adjust the cooking timer to 40 minutes.
4. Once the pressure cooker beeps, do quick pressure release to open the lid.
5. Press the Meat/Chicken button and add the egg noodles and sour cream. Cook without the lid on

until the noodles are done.

6. Press the Cancel/Keep Warm button to turn off the pressure cooker.

Simple Roast Beef with Gravy

Serving size: 8

Preparation time: 5 minutes

Cooking time: 50 minutes

Ingredients:
- 3-pounds rib-eye roast
- Salt and pepper to taste
- 1 shallot, chopped
- ½ bottle drinking red wine
- 5 cups beef stock

Instruction:
1. Press the Meat/Chicken button on the Power Pressure Cooker XL.
2. Season the steak with salt and pepper.
3. Sear and slightly brown each side for 3 minutes.
4. Add the shallots and cook until they are caramelized.
5. Mix in the rest of the ingredients.
6. Close the lid and adjust the cooking time to 40 minutes.
7. Do quick pressure release to open the lid.

8. Continue cooking without the lid on to thicken the sauce.

9. Press the Cancel/Keep Warm button once the sauce has thickened.

Sweet-Style Corned Beef

Serving size: 6

Preparation time: 5 minutes

Cooking time: 45 minutes

Ingredients:

- 2 pounds corned beef cut
- 1 cup prepared BBQ sauce
- 1 teaspoon rosemary
- ½ cup Worcestershire sauce
- ½ cup apple juice

Instruction:

1. Place all ingredients in the Power Pressure Cooker XL.
2. Close the lid and press the Meat/Chicken button.
3. Adjust the cooking timer to 40 minutes.
4. Once the pressure cooker beeps, do quick pressure release to open the lid.
5. Transfer the beef to a bowl and shred using fork.
6. Place it back to the pressure cooker.
7. Press the Meat/Chicken button again and cook without the lid on to reduce the sauce.

Side Dishes Recipes

Cheesy Cheddar Spirals

Serving size: 15

Preparation time: 10 minutes

Cooking time: 15 minutes

Ingredients:

- ½ cup butter
- 1 package spiral pasta
- 2 cups half-and-half cream
- 1 can cheddar cheese soup
- 4 cups mozzarella cheese, shredded

Instruction:

1. Press the Rice/Risotto button of the Power Pressure Cooker XL.
2. Heat the butter and add the spiral pasta. Mix for 1 minute until well combined.
3. Add the cream and cheddar cheese soup. Continue stirring until everything is incorporated.

4. Top with mozzarella cheese.

5. Close the lid and adjust the cooking time to 15 minutes.

6. Once the pressure cooker beeps, let the pressure release naturally to open the lid.

7. Serve warm.

Simplified Baked Potatoes

Serving size: 4

Preparation time: 2 minutes

Cooking time: 15 minutes

Ingredients:

- 4 medium-sized Russet potatoes, scrubbed and washed

Instruction:

1. Poke the potatoes with a fork for a few times and wrap them in aluminum foil.
2. Place a steamer rack in the Power Pressure Cooker XL and add 1 ½ cups of water.
3. Place the potatoes on the rack.
4. Close the lid and select the Meat/Chicken button.
5. Cook for 15 minutes.
6. Do quick pressure release to open the lid.
7. Serve with butter.

Nutrient-Dense Cauliflower Cheese

Serving size: 4

Preparation time: 5 minutes

Cooking time: 10 minutes

Ingredients:

- 2 cups cauliflower, cut into florets
- 2 cans cheddar cheese soup
- Salt and pepper to taste
- 1 cup cheddar cheese, shredded

Instruction:

1. Place the cauliflower florets and cheddar cheese soup in the Power Pressure Cooker XL.
2. Season with salt and pepper. Add in the cheese. Mix until well combined.
3. Close the lid and press the Fish/Vegetable/Steam button.
4. Adjust the cooking timer to 10 minutes.
5. Once the pressure cooker beeps, do quick pressure release to open the lid.

Effortless Steamed Corn

Serving size: 6

Preparation time: 5 minutes

Cooking time: 15 minutes

Ingredients:

- 6 halves of corn on the cob
- ¼ cup softened butter
- Salt and pepper to taste

Instruction:

1. Coat the corn with butter.
2. Season with salt and pepper if needed.
3. Wrap the corn in aluminum foil individually.
4. Place a steamer rack in the Power Pressure Cooker XL.
5. Add 1 ½ cup of water.
6. Place the corn in the pressure cooker and press the Fish/Vegetable/Steam button.
7. Adjust the cooking time to 15 minutes
8. Release the pressure immediately.
9. Serve hot.

Healthy BBQ Beans

Serving size: 6

Preparation time: 5 minutes

Cooking time: 20 minutes

Ingredients:

- 1 pound bacon, chopped
- 1 large can of baked beans
- 1 bottle of your favorite barbecue sauce
- 1 packet of ranch seasoning
- 1 cup brown sugar

Instruction:

1. Place all ingredients the Power Pressure Cooker XL.
2. Mix until well combined.
3. Close the lid and press the Bean/Lentil button.
4. Adjust the cooking timer to 20 minutes.
5. Once the pressure cooker beeps, let the pressure release naturally.

Light And Creamy Cheesy Tortellini

Serving size: 6

Preparation time: 5 minutes

Cooking time: 15 minutes

Ingredients:

- 1 package cheese tortellini
- 1 jar tomato and basil pasta sauce
- 4 cups mozzarella cheese, shredded
- ½ teaspoon garlic powder
- 2 teaspoon dried basil leaves

Instruction:

1. Place all ingredients in the Power Pressure Cooker XL. Mix until well combined.
2. Close the lid and press the Rice/Risotto button.
3. Adjust the cooking time to 15 minutes.
4. Once it is done, release the pressure naturally.

Garlicky Buttery Greens

Serving size: 8

Preparation time: 5 minutes

Cooking time: 2 minutes

Ingredients:

- 3 tablespoon butter
- 3 teaspoon garlic powder
- 1 pound green beans, trimmed and snapped
- Salt and pepper to taste

Instruction:

1. In a mixing bowl, toss all ingredients together.
2. Place in an aluminum foil and seal the edges.
3. Place a steamer rack in the Power Pressure Cooker XL.
4. Add 1 cup water.
5. Press the Fish/Vegetable/Steam button and cook on preset cooking time.
6. Do quick pressure release to open the lid and take out the vegetables.

Glazed Sweet Carrots

Serving size: 8

Preparation time: 5 minutes

Cooking time: 10 minutes

Ingredients:

- 2-pounds carrots, peeled and cut into strips
- Salt and pepper to taste
- ¼ cup butter
- ¼ cup brown sugar

Instruction:

1. In a mixing bowl, toss all ingredients together.
2. Place in an aluminum foil and seal the edges.
3. Place a steamer rack in the Power Pressure Cooker XL.
4. Add 1 ½ cup water.
5. Press the Fish/Vegetable/Steam button.
6. Adjust the cooking time to 10 minutes.
7. Do quick pressure release to open the lid and take out the vegetables.

Chicken Recipes

Carolina Sweet-Style BBQ Chicken

Serving size: 6

Preparation time: 5 minutes

Cooking time: 25 minutes

Ingredients:

- 2 cups chicken broth
- 1 cup white vinegar
- ¼ cup sugar
- 1 ½ pounds boneless chicken breast
- ¾ teaspoon salt

Instruction:

1. Place all ingredients in a mixing bowl. Marinate for at least 2 hours in the refrigerator.
2. After two hours, place all ingredients in the Power Pressure Cooker XL.
3. Close the lid and press the Meat/Chicken button.
4. Adjust the cooking time to 25 minutes.

5. Do quick pressure release once the pressure cooker beeps.
6. Press the Meat/Chicken button again and continue cooking without the lid on to reduce the sauce.

Scrumptious Buffalo Ranch Chicken

Serving size: 5

Preparation time: 5 minutes

Cooking time: 20 minutes

Ingredients:

- 5-pieces boneless chicken breasts
- 1 packet ranch seasoning mix
- 1 bottle packaged buffalo sauce
- 1 teaspoon rosemary

Instruction:

1. Place all ingredients in the Power Pressure Cooker XL.
2. Close the lid and press the Meat/Chicken button.
3. Adjust the cooking time to 15 minutes.
4. Do quick pressure release once the pressure cooker beeps.
5. Press the Meat/Chicken button again and continue cooking without the lid on to reduce the sauce.

Pressure-Steamed Chicken with Onion Ranch Sauce

Serving size: 12
Preparation time: 2 hours
Cooking time: 40 minutes

Ingredients:

- 1 packet of onion soup powder
- 1 packet ranch dressing mix
- 3 tablespoon garlic powder
- 1 teaspoon paprika
- 1 whole chicken (approximately 5 pounds), sliced into different segments

Instruction:

1. In a small mixing bowl, mix together the first four ingredients to make a dry rub.
2. Pour the dry rub mixture over the chicken pieces and mix until well combined. Place in the fridge to marinate for at least 2 hours.
3. Add a steamer rack in the Power Pressure Cooker

XL. Pour 2 cups of water.

4. Place the chicken pieces in a heat-proof dish and cover with aluminum foil. Place on the steamer rack.

5. Close the lid and press the Meat/Chicken button.

6. Adjust the cooking time to 40 minutes.

7. Do quick pressure release once the pressure cooker beeps.

General Tso's Chicken With A Zing

Serving size: 6

Preparation time: 5 minutes

Cooking time: 20 minutes

Ingredients:

- 4 boneless chicken breasts
- 1 bottle of prepared General Tsao stir fry sauce
- 8 dried chilies (preferably Thai chilies)
- 2 green onions, chopped finely
- A dash of sesame seeds for garnish

Instruction:

1. Place all ingredients except the sesame seeds in the Power Pressure Cooker XL.
2. Close the lid and press the Meat/Chicken button.
3. Adjust the cooking time to 15 minutes.
4. Do quick pressure release once the pressure cooker beeps.
5. Press the Meat/Chicken button again and continue cooking without the lid on to reduce the sauce.
6. Sprinkle with sesame seeds as toppings.

Garlicky and Lemony Chicken

Serving size: 4

Preparation time: 5 minutes

Cooking time: 20 minutes

Ingredients:

- 4 boneless chicken breast
- 1 can cream of mushroom soup
- 1 can cream of chicken soup
- 1 lemon, juiced
- 4 cloves of garlic, minced

Instruction:

1. Place all ingredients in the Power Pressure Cooker XL.
2. Close the lid and make sure that it is locked in place.
3. Press the Meat/Chicken button and adjust the cooking time to 15 minutes.
4. Do quick pressure release once the pressure cooker beeps.
5. Press the Meat/Chicken button again and continue cooking without the lid on to reduce the sauce.

Moist And Juicy Chicken Breasts

Serving size: 8

Preparation time: 5 minutes

Cooking time: 15 minutes

Ingredients:

- 8 chicken breasts
- ½ cup water
- 2 tablespoon brown sugar
- Salt and pepper to taste
- A sprig of fresh rosemary

Instruction:

1. Place all ingredients in the Power Pressure Cooker XL.
2. Close the lid and make sure that the lid is secure.
3. Press the Meat/Chicken button.
4. Adjust the cooking time to 15 minutes.
5. Do quick pressure release once the pressure cooker beeps.

Tropical Luau Chicken

Serving size: 6

Preparation time: 5 minutes

Cooking time: 20 minutes

Ingredients:

- 6 bacon, chopped
- 6 boneless chicken thighs
- Salt and pepper to taste
- 1 cup crushed pineapple
- ¾ cup barbecue sauce

Instruction:

1. Press the Meat/Chicken button on the Power Pressure Cooker XL.
2. Add the bacon and cook until crispy. Set aside half of the bacon for garnish later.
3. Add the chicken and season with salt and pepper to taste.
4. Cook for 3 minutes on each side until slightly golden brown.
5. Add the pineapples and barbecue sauce.

6. Close the lid and make sure that the lid is secure.

7. Press the Meat/Chicken button

8. Adjust the cooking time to 15 minutes.

9. Do quick pressure release once the pressure cooker beeps.

10. Sprinkle with the remaining bacon bits for added crunch.

Special Southwest Chicken

Serving size: 6

Preparation time: 5 minutes

Cooking time: 15 minutes

Ingredients:

- 1 can black beans, rinsed and rained
- 1 jar salsa
- 1 can whole kernel corn, drained
- 4 boneless chicken breast

Instruction:

1. Place all ingredients in the Power Pressure Cooker XL.
2. Close the lid and make sure that the lid is secure.
3. Press the Meat/Chicken button.
4. Adjust the cooking time to 15 minutes.
5. Do quick pressure release once the pressure cooker beeps.
6. Garnish with yellow pepper strips, sour cream, or cheddar cheese if desired.

Oriental Mandarin Chicken

Serving size: 4

Preparation time: 5 minutes

Cooking time: 20 minutes

Ingredients:

- 4 boneless chicken breasts
- 10 ounces of prepared Mandarin sauce
- Salt and pepper to taste
- ½ cup pineapple preserves

Instruction:

1. Place all ingredients in the Power Pressure Cooker XL.
2. Close the lid and press the Meat/Chicken button.
3. Adjust the cooking time to 15 minutes.
4. Do quick pressure release once the pressure cooker beeps.
5. Press the Meat/Chicken button again and cook without the lid on to reduce the sauce.

Sweet Hawaiian Chicken

Serving size: 4

Preparation time: 5 minutes

Cooking time: 15 minutes

Ingredients:

- 4 boneless chicken breast
- 1 bottle Hawaiian-style barbecue sauce
- 1 can pineapple chunks
- Salt and pepper to taste

Instruction:

1. Place all ingredients in the Power Pressure Cooker XL.
2. Close the lid and press the Meat/Chicken button.
3. Cook using the preset cooking time.
4. Do quick pressure release once the pressure cooker beeps.
5. Press the Meat/Chicken button again and cook without the lid on to reduce the sauce.

Sweet-Style Teriyaki Chicken

Serving size: 4

Preparation time: 30 minutes

Cooking time: 15 minutes

Ingredients:

- 4 boneless chicken breast
- 1 bottle prepared teriyaki sauce
- 1 teaspoon brown sugar
- 1 tablespoon sesame oil
- 1 sprig green onions, chopped

Instruction:

1. Mix all ingredients in a mixing bowl and marinate for at least 30 minutes.
2. Place the marinated chicken in the Power Pressure Cooker XL.
3. Close the lid and press the Meat/Chicken button.
4. Cook using the preset cooking time.
5. Do quick pressure release once the pressure cooker beeps.

Spicy Chipotle Chicken

Serving size: 4

Preparation time: 5 minutes

Cooking time: 20 minutes

Ingredients:

- 4 boneless chicken breast
- 1 cup chipotle barbecue sauce
- 1 cup peach preserves
- Salt and pepper to taste

Instruction:

1. Place all ingredients in the Power Pressure Cooker XL.
2. Close the lid and press the Meat/Chicken button.
3. Cook using the preset cooking time.
4. Do quick pressure release once the pressure cooker beeps.
5. Press the Meat/Chicken button again and cook without the lid on to reduce the sauce.
6. Serve with corn or mashed potatoes as side dish.

Easy Sweet and Sour Chicken

Serving size: 4

Preparation time: 5 minutes

Cooking time: 20 minutes

Ingredients:

- 4 boneless chicken breast
- ¾ cup chicken broth
- ¼ cup apple cider vinegar
- ¾ cup sugar
- Salt and pepper

Instruction:

1. Place all ingredients in the Power Pressure Cooker XL.
2. Close the lid and press the Meat/Chicken button.
3. Adjust the cooking to 15 minutes.
4. Do quick pressure release once the pressure cooker beeps.
5. Press the Meat/Chicken button again and cook without the lid on to reduce the sauce or you can add a cornstarch slurry to thicken the sauce

immediately.

6. Serve with rice.

Asian-Style Orange Chicken

Serving size: 4

Preparation time: 5 minutes

Cooking time: 15 minutes

Ingredients:

- 4 boneless chicken breast
- ¾ cup orange marmalade
- ¾ cup barbecue sauce
- 2 tablespoon soy sauce
- ¼ cup water

Instruction:

1. Place all ingredients in the Power Pressure Cooker XL.
2. Close the lid and press the Meat/Chicken button.
3. Adjust the cooking to 15 minutes.
4. Do quick pressure release once the pressure cooker beeps.

Garlicky Parmesan Chicken

Serving size: 4

Preparation time: 5 minutes

Cooking time: 15 minutes

Ingredients:

- 4 boneless chicken breast
- 2 sticks butter
- 1 cup mayonnaise
- 1 cup parmesan cheese
- 3 tablespoon garlic powder

Instruction:

1. Place all ingredients in the Power Pressure Cooker XL.
2. Close the lid and press the Meat/Chicken button.
3. Adjust the cooking to 15 minutes.
4. Do quick pressure release once the pressure cooker beeps.

Made in the USA
Lexington, KY
11 June 2017